Men's Edition

2nd Edition

21st Century Musica[l]

50 Songs from Shows Since

C000127975

ISBN 978-1-4803-9625-8

HAL•LEONARD®

7777 W. BLUEMOUND RD. P.O. BOX 13819 MILWAUKEE, WI 53213

Visit Hal Leonard Online at
www.halleonard.com

CONTENTS
Alphabetically by Show Title

CONTENTS
Alphabetically by Song Title

PROUD OF YOUR BOY

from *Aladdin*

Music by Alan Menken
Lyrics by Howard Ashman

With determination, poco rubato

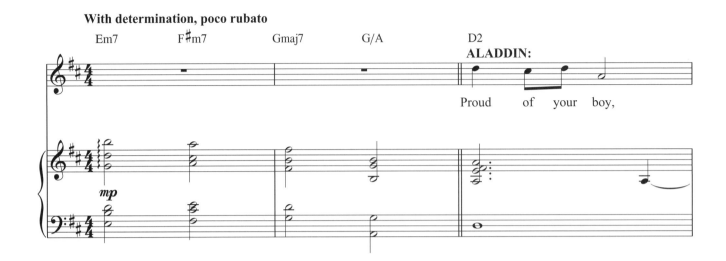

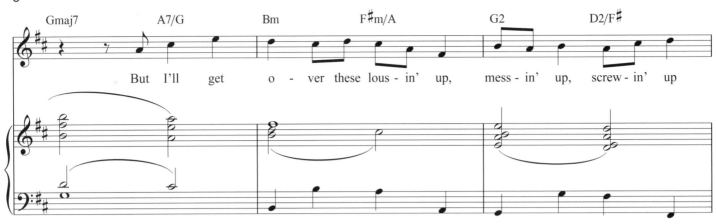

But I'll get o - ver these lous - in' up, mess - in' up, screw - in' up

times. You'll see, Ma, now comes the bet - ter part.

Some one's gon - na make good, cross his stu - pid heart... Make good and

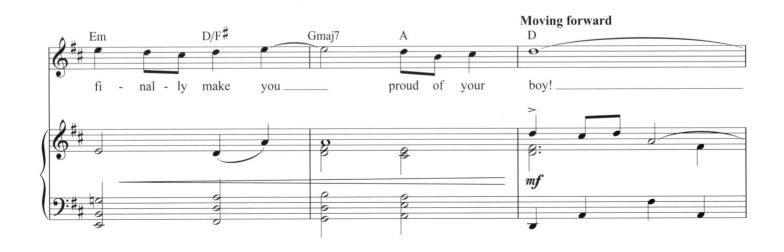

fi - nal - ly make you proud of your boy!

Moving forward

STILL
from *Anastasia*

Lyrics by Lynn Ahrens
Music by Stephen Flaherty

IF YOU WERE GAY
from the Broadway Musical *Avenue Q*

Music and Lyrics by Robert Lopez
and Jeff Marx

free to ___ say that I was gay! (But I'm not gay!)

If you were

queer, I'd still be here, year af - ter

year, be - cause you're dear to ___ me. And I know that

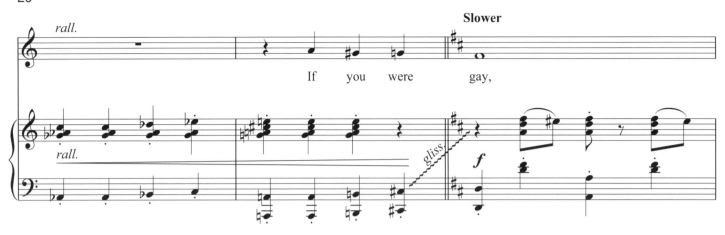

If you were gay,

I'd shout hoo - ray! And here I'd

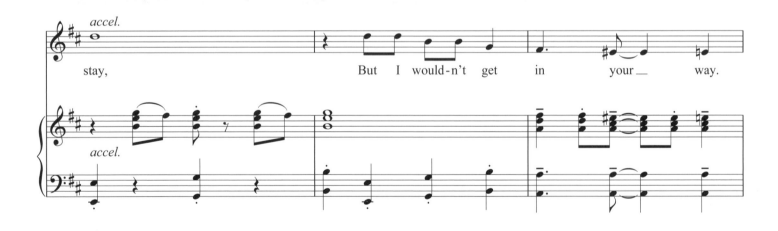

stay, But I would-n't get in your __ way.

You can count on me to al - ways

I'M NOT WEARING UNDERWEAR TODAY

from the Broadway Musical *Avenue Q*

Music and Lyrics by Robert Lopez
and Jeff Marx

Fast and circus-like

BRIAN:

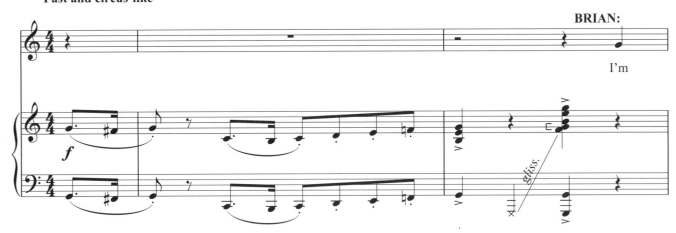

PURPOSE
from the Broadway Musical *Avenue Q*

Music and Lyrics by Robert Lopez
and Jeff Marx

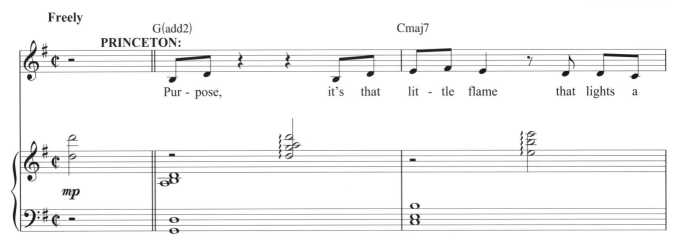

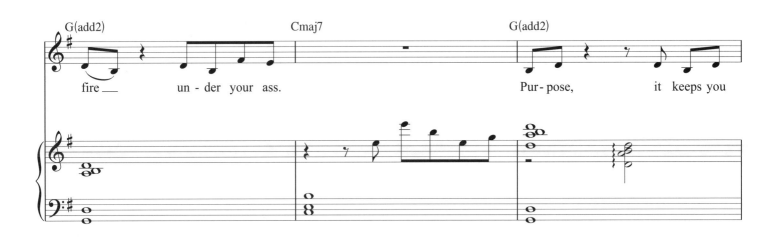

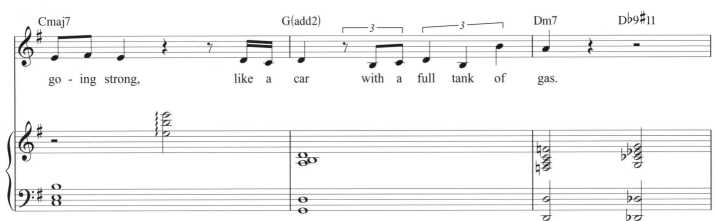

Princeton is joined by Moving Boxes in this song, adapted here as a solo.

FIGHT THE DRAGONS

from *Big Fish*

Music and Lyrics by
Andrew Lippa

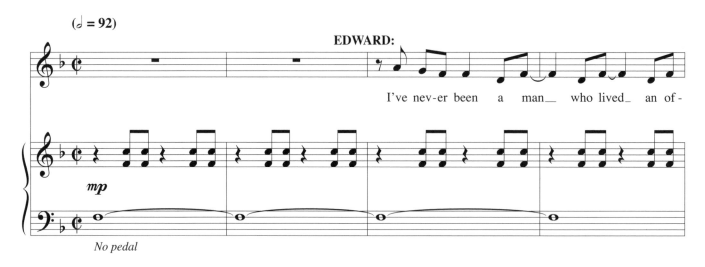

make a friend,__ and pray the day__ will nev - er end,__ 'cuz there's one more ad - ven -

- ture wait-in' 'round__ an-oth-er bend__ where I fight the__ drag -

mf as before

Pedal okay

- ons and I storm the__ cas - tles and I win a__ bat -

- tle or__ two.__ But then a feel - ing__ comes,__

boy in - to_____ a big - ger man.

rit.

So I'll fight the__ drag -

ons_____ 'til__ you can._____

STRANGER
from *Big Fish*

Music and Lyrics by
Andrew Lippa

But still feels_ true.   I'm

pass-ing through_ a rite_ that ev - 'ry par-ent does._   I'm

walk-ing on___ some shared_ fa - mil - iar ground.____   Yet

ev-'ry step_ I take_ is not a step that was._   And I've

What do I feel?_____ I

feel con-nect -ed in a way_ I've nev - er known.__ A

line from Dad_ to me_ to new - born son. So from to-day_ I'll nev-er make_ a

choice a-lone.__ One for all, all for one. And

when he's born,_ I'll teach him how_ to use__ his com-mon sense._ He'll

lis-ten and_ he'll learn_ and he'll_ ex - cel.__ I'll

tell my son_ that life is lived_ in clear and pres-ent tense,_ not on-

- ly in__ the sto_ ries we_ can tell.__ My

fa - ther told me sto-ries I could nev-er com-pre-hend._____ In

ev-'ry tale__ he'd claim__ to be__ the he - ro._____ I've

Broadly

tried to un-der-stand__ him,__ but I won-der if I__ can. Be-cause af-ter al-most thir-ty years,__ I

a tempo

still don't know the man._____ I

I BELIEVE
from the Broadway Musical *The Book of Mormon*

Words and Music by Trey Parker,
Robert Lopez and Matt Stone
Vocal Arrangement by Stephen Oremus

Chorus parts have been omitted from this solo voice edition.

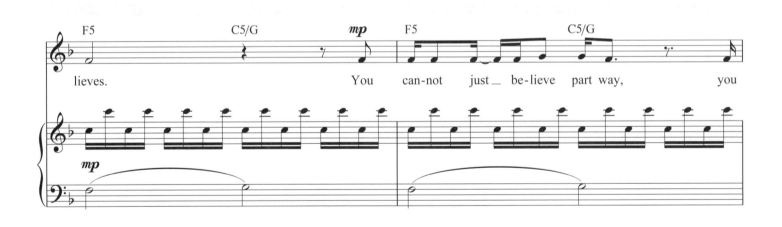

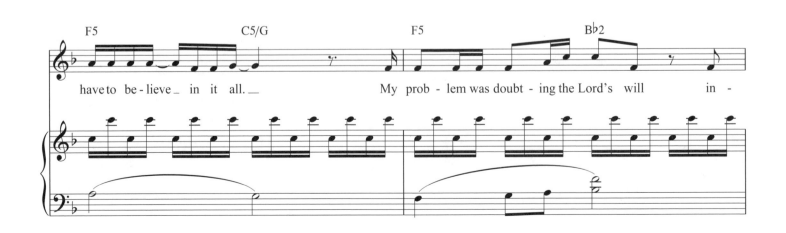

IT ALL FADES AWAY
from *The Bridges of Madison County*

Music and Lyrics by
Jason Robert Brown

SOMEONE ELSE'S SKIN
from *Catch Me If You Can*

Lyrics by Scott Wittman and Marc Shaiman
Music by Marc Shaiman

* The spoken lines may be omitted for a solo performance.

FOR FOREVER
from *Dear Evan Hansen*

Music and Lyrics by Benj Pasek
and Justin Paul

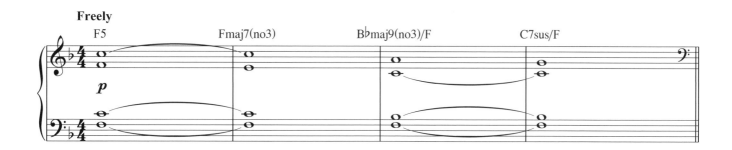

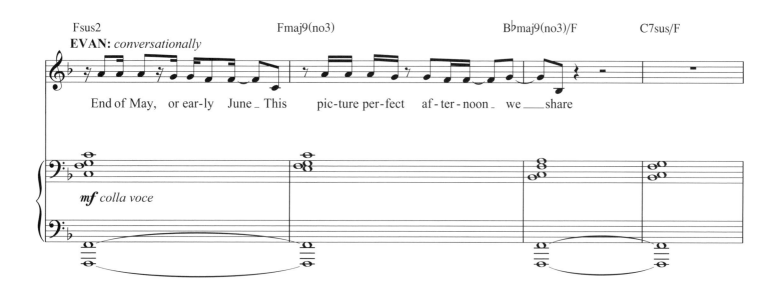

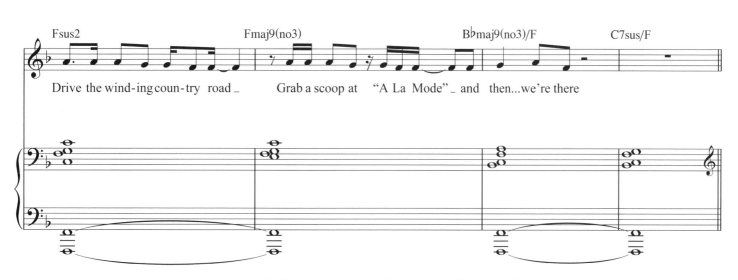

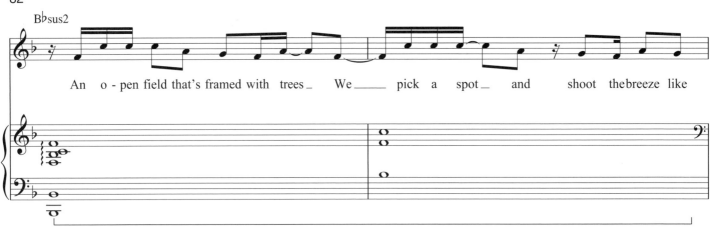

An o-pen field that's framed with trees __ We____ pick a spot__ and shoot the breeze like

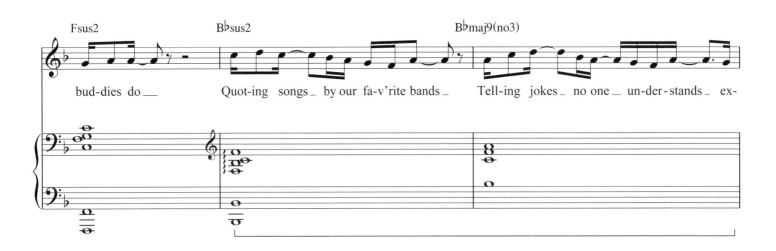

bud-dies do __ Quot-ing songs __ by our fa-v'rite bands __ Tell-ing jokes __ no one __ un-der-stands __ ex-

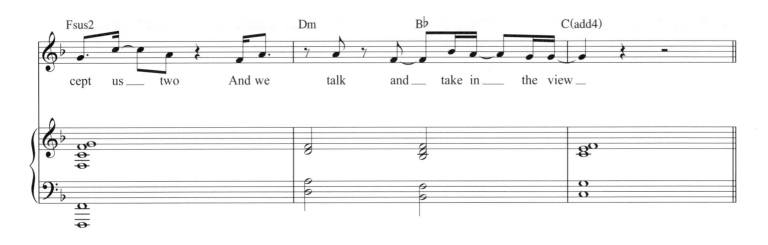

cept us __ two And we talk and __ take in __ the view __

All____ we see is __ sky ____ for for-ev-er We ___

With pedal

WAVING THROUGH A WINDOW

from *Dear Evan Hansen*

Music and Lyrics by Benj Pasek
and Justin Paul

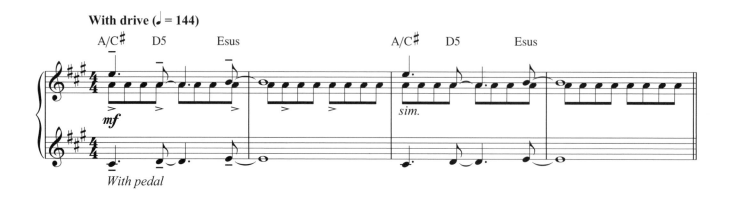

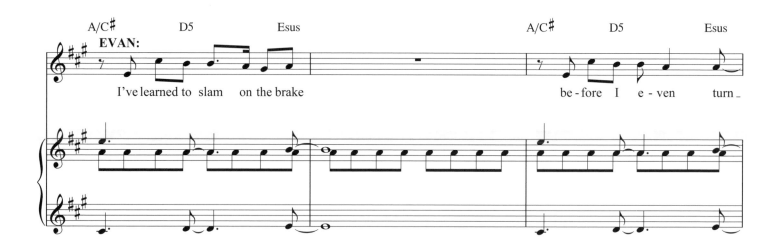

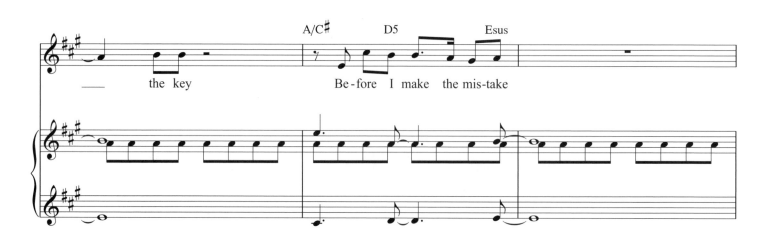

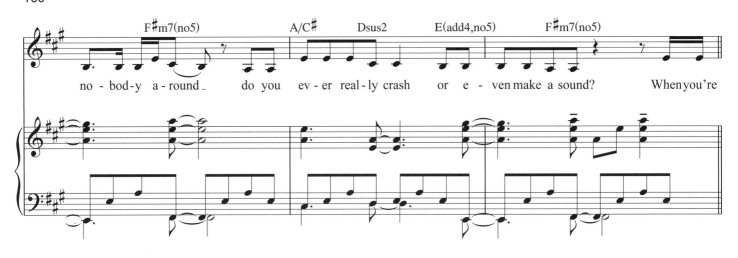

no - bod-y a - round __ do you ev - er real - ly crash or e - ven make a sound? When you're

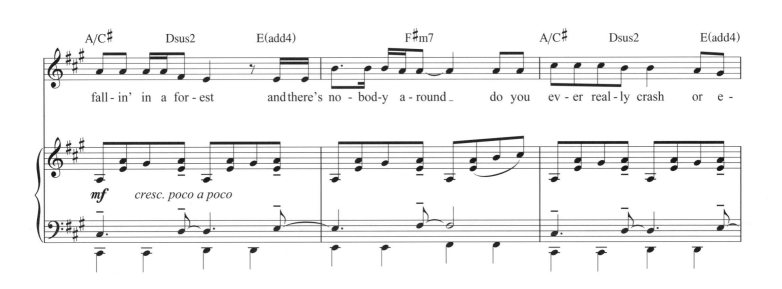

fall - in' in a for - est and there's no - bod-y a - round __ do you ev - er real - ly crash or e -

(EVAN:) ven make a sound? __ When you're fall - in' in a for - est and there's no - bod y a - round __ Do you

COMPANY: Ah ___

Ah ___

GREAT BIG STUFF
from *Dirty Rotten Scoundrels*

Words and Music by
David Yazbek

Freddy is accompanied by ensemble, eliminated in this solo edition.

This phrase, sung by ensemble in the show, can be sung one octave higher by Freddy from this point on, each time it occurs.

I AM ALDOLPHO
from *The Drowsy Chaperone*

Words and Music by Lisa Lambert
and Greg Morrison

Bright Paso Doble

ALDOLPHO:

I'm

A Tempo (tango, in 4)

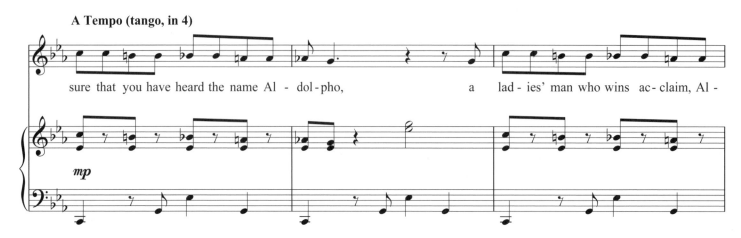

sure that you have heard the name Al - dol - pho,   a lad - ies' man who wins ac - claim, Al -

IN LOVE WITH YOU
from the Musical *First Date*

Music and Lyrics by
Alan Zachary and Michael Weiner

IN SUMMER
from *Frozen*

Music and Lyrics by Kristen Anderson-Lopez
and Robert Lopez

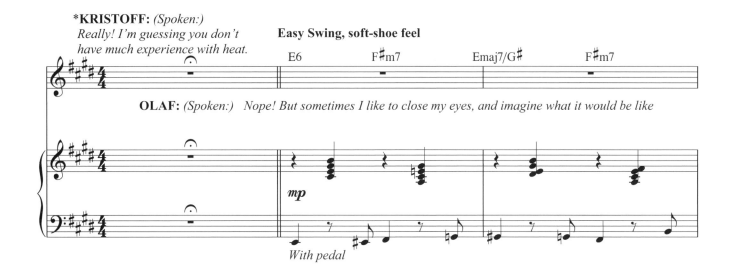

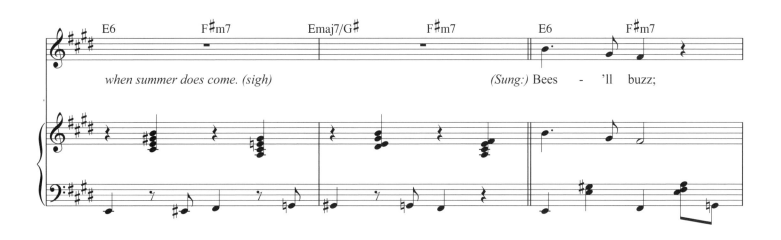

*Spoken dialogue may be omitted for a solo performance.

MAN

from *The Full Monty*

Words and Music by
David Yazbek

This version has been adapted as a solo.

8vb throughout

tough. Your smell is scar-y. Here's what you're not you're not a

fair-y. No you're a beer drink-in' real live ___ man.

loco

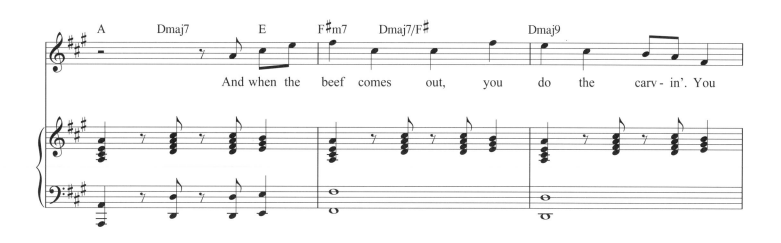

And when the beef comes out, you do the carv-in'. You

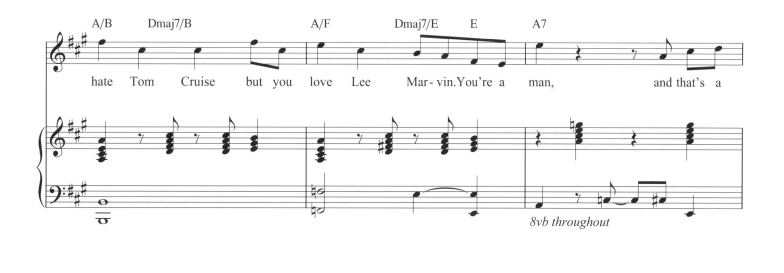

hate Tom Cruise but you love Lee Mar-vin. You're a man, and that's a

8vb throughout

* air guitar this Led Zeppelin lick

FOOLISH TO THINK
from *A Gentleman's Guide to Love & Murder*

Music by Steven Lutvak
Lyrics by Robert L. Freedman and
Steven Lutvak

*Measures 86–101 were cut for the Broadway production. Cut to **

SIBELLA
from *A Gentleman's Guide to Love & Murder*

Music by Steven Lutvak
Lyrics by Robert L. Freedman and
Steven Lutvak

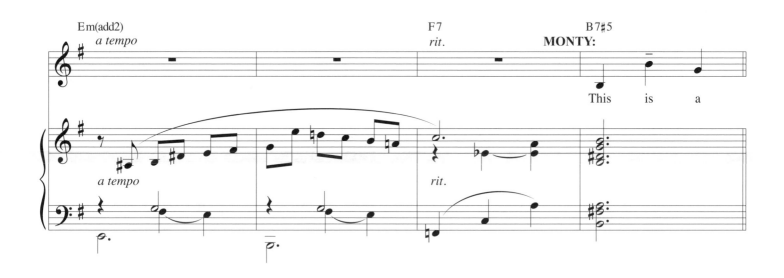

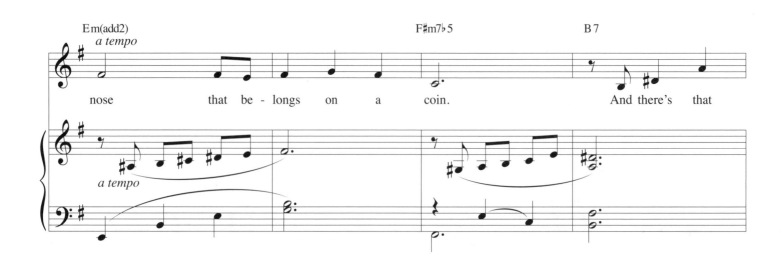

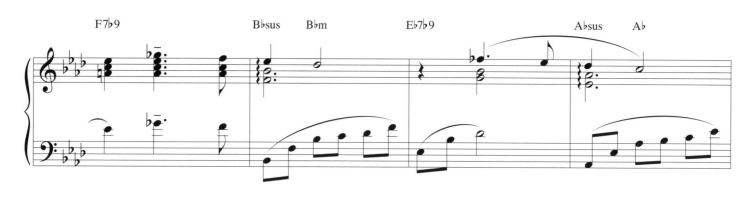

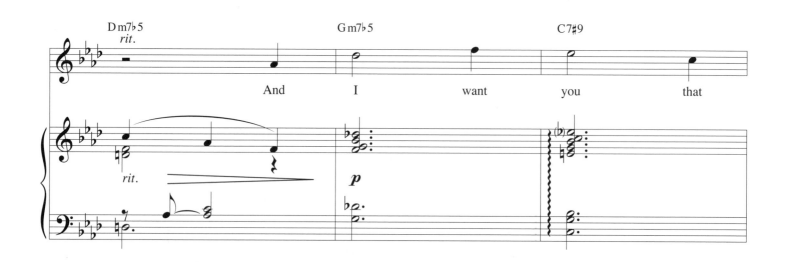

YOU'LL BE BACK

from *Hamilton*

Words and Music by
Lin-Manuel Miranda

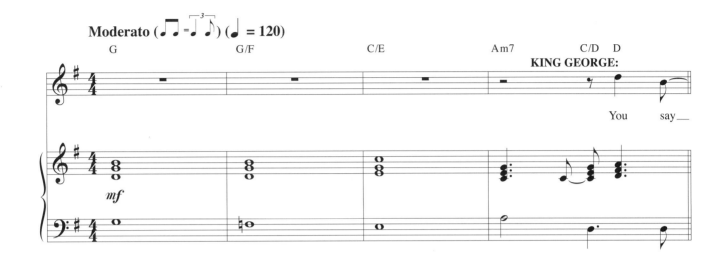

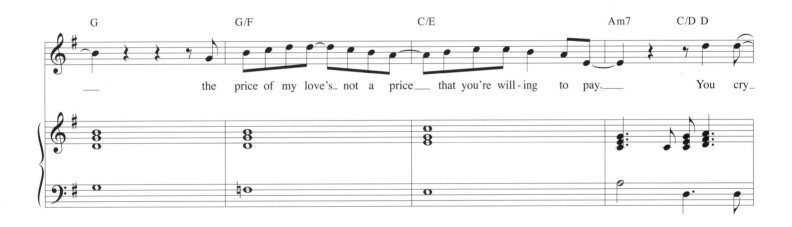

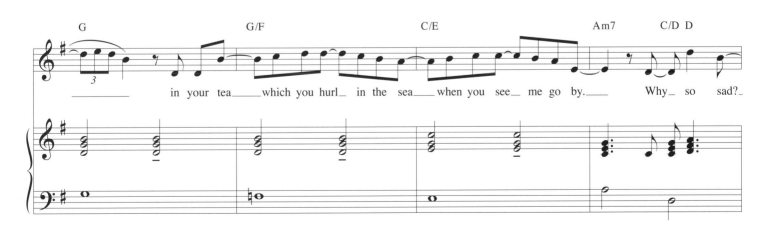

159

* Ensemble may be omitted for a Solo performance.

ISN'T THAT ENOUGH?

from *Honeymoon in Vegas*

Music and Lyrics by
Jason Robert Brown

A little more movement

She likes my cook-ing At least she tries. She thinks I'm fun-ny. When I get cra-zy, she nev-er cries, We work things through. And she in-spires me like no one does. She makes me bet-ter than I was. Is-n't that e-nough for

This page has been intentionally left blank to facilitate page turns.

YOU DON'T NEED TO LOVE ME

from *If/Then*

Lyrics by Brian Yorkey
Music by Tom Kitt

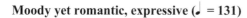

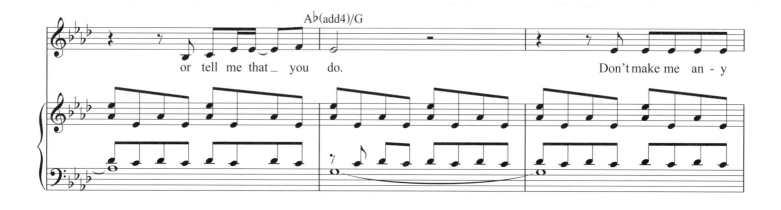

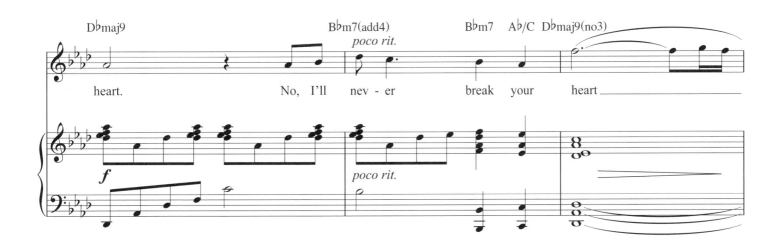

You don't need to love me to let me help you

through. You don't need to con - fide in me—

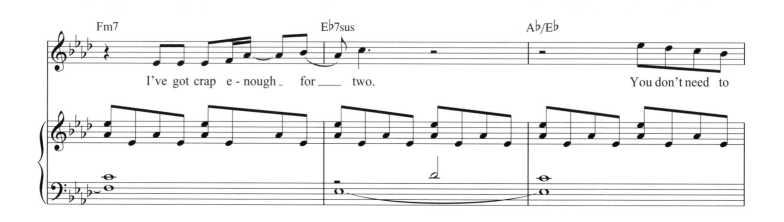

I've got crap e - nough for two. You don't need to

an - swer, I'll know be - fore you do...

But hear me, ___ and be - lieve me, ___

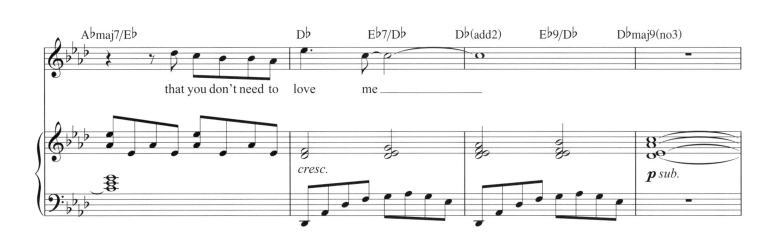

that you don't need to love me ___

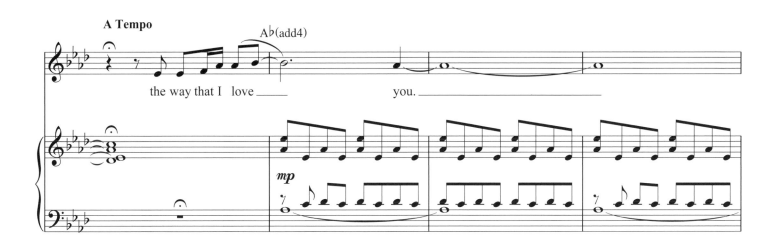

the way that I love ___ you. ___

STEP ONE
from the Broadway Musical *Kinky Boots*

Words and Music by
Cynthia Lauper

IF I DIDN'T BELIEVE IN YOU
from *The Last Five Years*

Music and Lyrics by
Jason Robert Brown

MOVING TOO FAST
from *The Last Five Years*

Music and Lyrics by
Jason Robert Brown

Two thous-and bucks with-out__ re - writ-ing one word!

I left Co - lum-bi - a and I don't re - gret it,

I wrote a book and Son - ny Meh - ta____ read it!

My heart's been sto - len! My____ e - go's swol - len! I__

SHIKSA GODDESS
from *The Last Five Years*

Music and Lyrics by
Jason Robert Brown

at__ your ser - vice! Just tell me what_ to

do!_____

I say, Hey hey hey hey!__ I've been

wait - ing__ for some - one, I've been pray - ing__ for some-

one, I think that I could be in love_____ with some -

- one_____ Like

you!_____

IL MONDO ERA VUOTO

from *The Light in the Piazza*

Words and Music by
Adam Guettel
Italian Translation by Judith Blazer

With Italian lyricism (Poco rubato)

FABRIZIO:

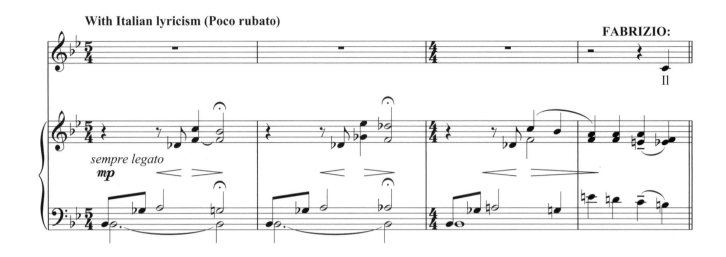

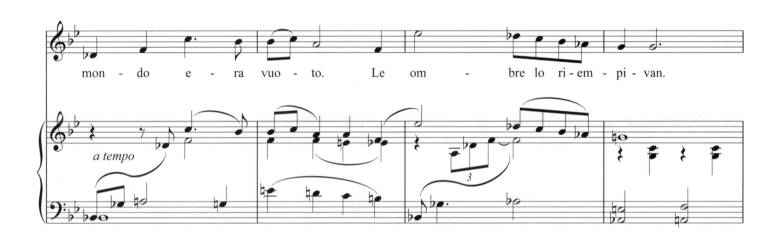

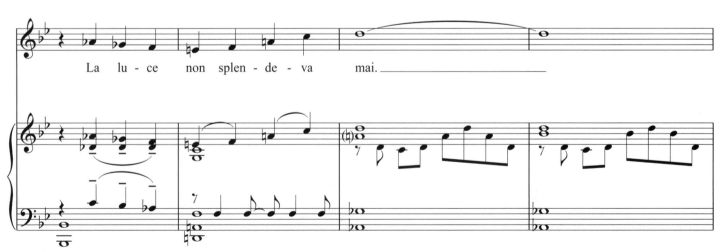

The song is a whole step lower on the cast recording. This higher key was subsequently provided by the composer for vocal comfortability in the role.

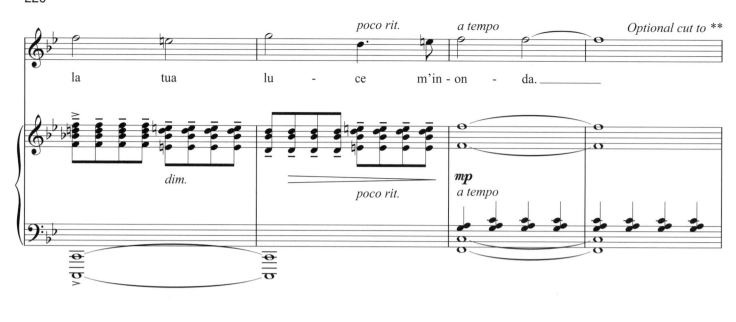

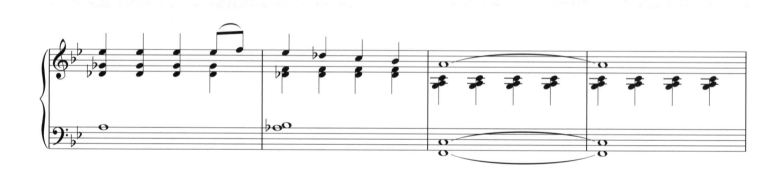

Ma lei non può a-mar-mi! Non co-sì! Oh Cla-ra! Non a-me-rà un ra-gaz-zi-no!

O di - o, dam - mi - la mia Cla - ra! _____

O Pa - dre la sua lu - ce... M'in - on - da.

LOVE TO ME
from *The Light in the Piazza*

Words and Music by
Adam Guettel

know that you are beau - ti - ful,

or that an - y - one_____ is_____ watch - ing you.

This is what I see._____

And I

no - tice how you hun - ger for sur - prise,_____

and do not think that you are tall e - nough,

like you're stand - ing on_____ a

moun - tain - side_____ a - lone._____ This is what I

see._____ Oh_____

Oh_____

_____ You're not_____ a - lone!_____

Now I see as I have nev-er seen_____ be -

TAKE A CHANCE ON ME
from the Stage Musical *Little Women*

Music by Jason Howland
Lyrics by Mindi Dickstein

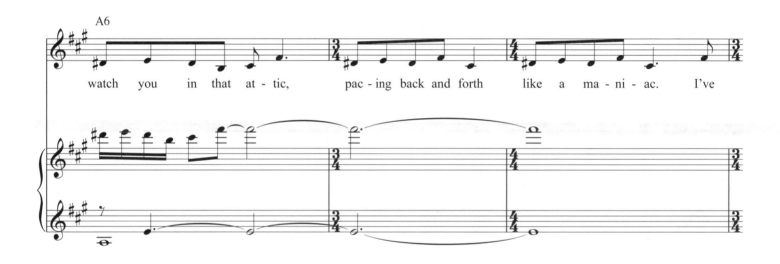

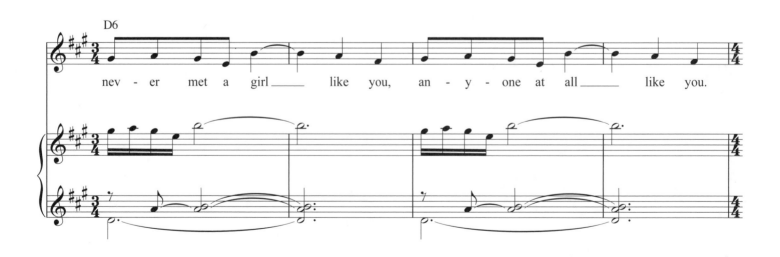

This is ver - y nice, such a love - ly par - ty. The mu - sic sounds so thrill - ing.

It makes a per - son feel like danc - ing.

(rhythmically steady)

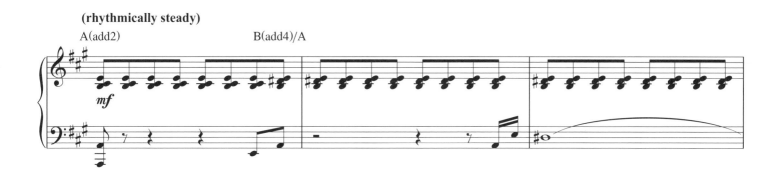

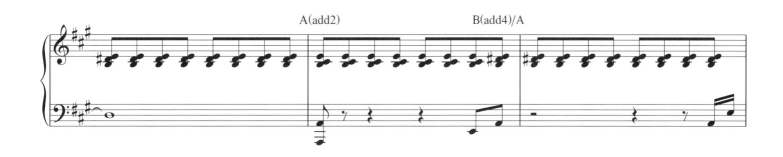

THE STREETS OF DUBLIN

from *A Man of No Importance*

Lyrics by Lynn Ahrens
Music by Stephen Flaherty

MEMPHIS LIVES IN ME

from *Memphis*

Music by David Bryan
Lyrics by Joe DiPietro
and David Bryan

Medium slow Ballad

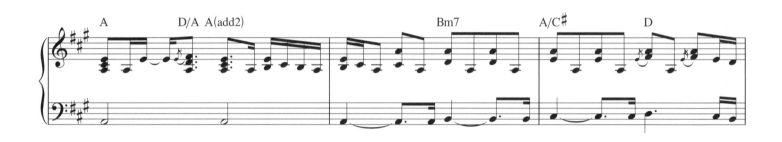

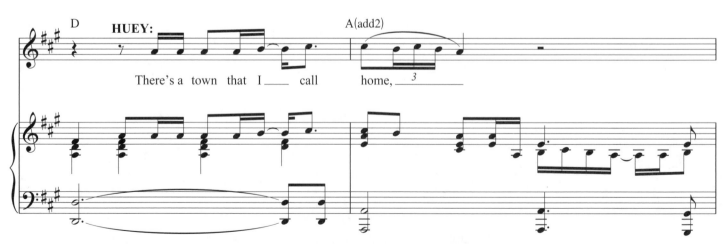

There's a town that I ___ call home, ___

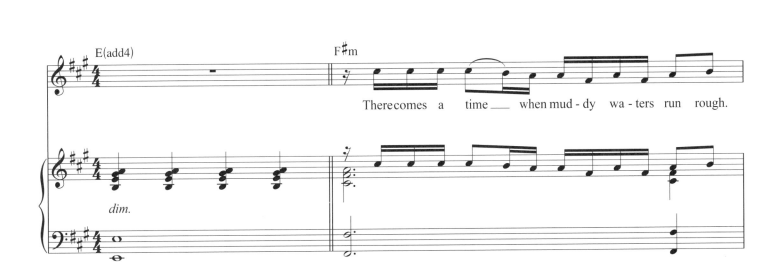

There comes a time ___ when mud - dy wa - ters run rough.

YOU WON'T SUCCEED
ON BROADWAY

from *Monty Python's Spamalot*

Lyrics by Eric Idle
Music by John Du Prez and Eric Idle

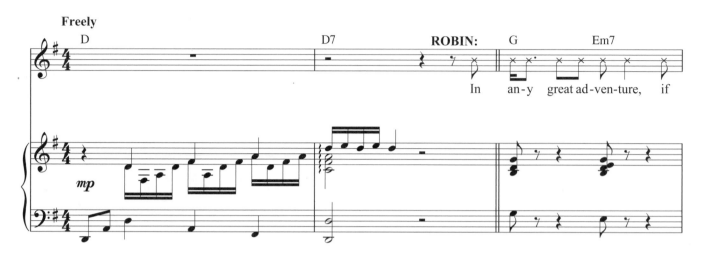

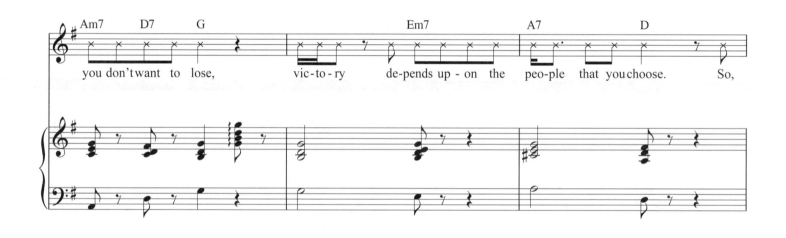

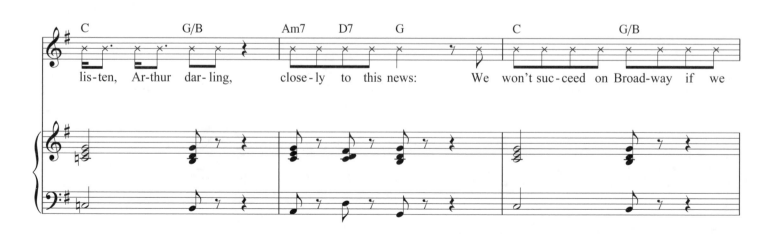

don't have an - y Jews.

You may

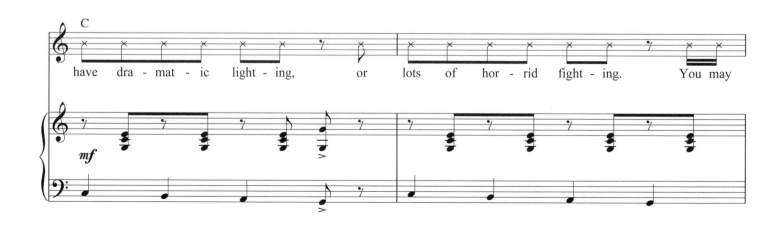

have dra - mat - ic light - ing, or lots of hor - rid fight - ing. You may

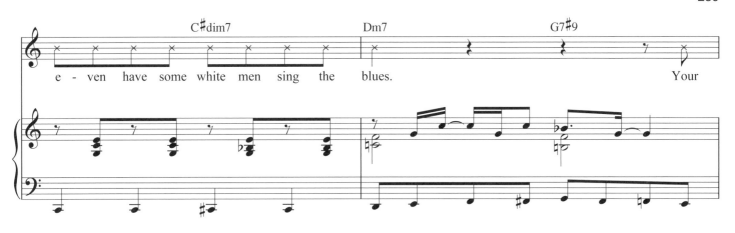

e - ven have some white men sing the blues.

Your

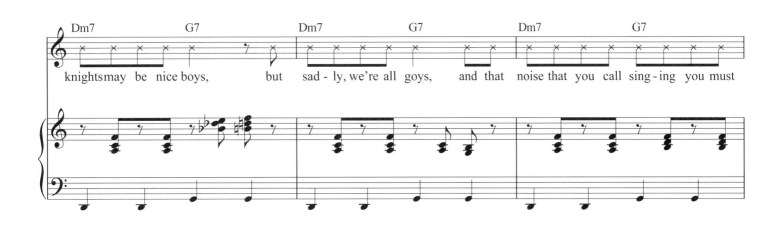

knights may be nice boys, but sad - ly, we're all goys, and that noise that you call sing - ing you must

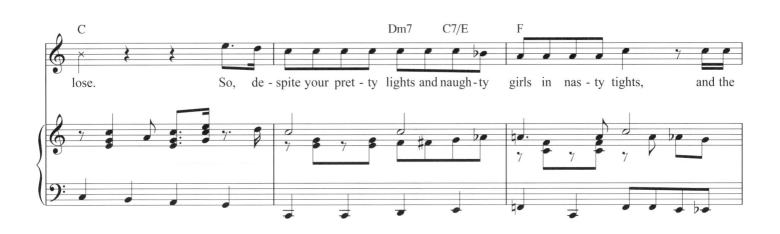

lose. So, de - spite your pret - ty lights and naugh - ty girls in nas - ty tights, and the

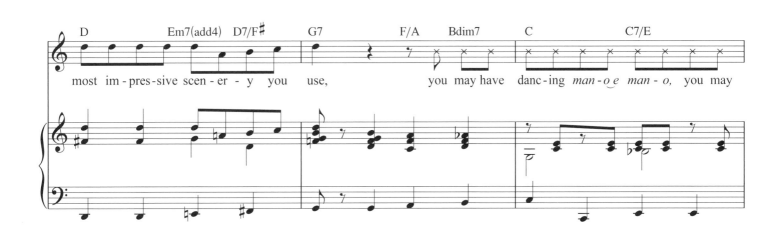

most im - pres - sive scen - er - y you use, you may have danc - ing *man - o e man - o,* you may

bring on a pi - an - o, but they will not give a damn-o if you don't have an - y Jews.

Looney Tunes

Hey!

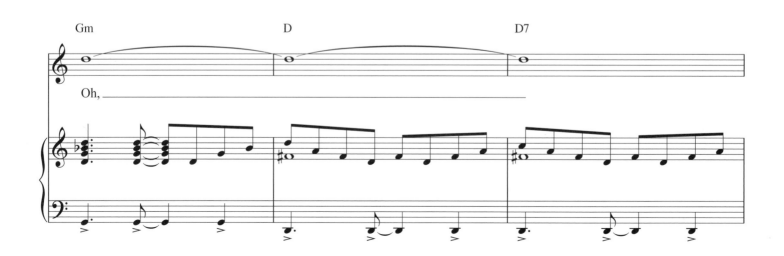

Oh, _____

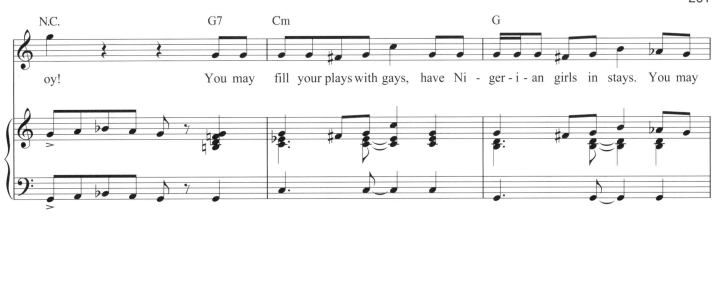

oy! You may fill your plays with gays, have Ni - ger - i - an girls in stays. You may

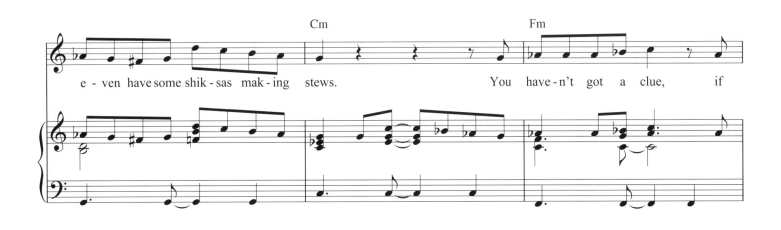

e - ven have some shik - sas mak - ing stews. You have-n't got a clue, if

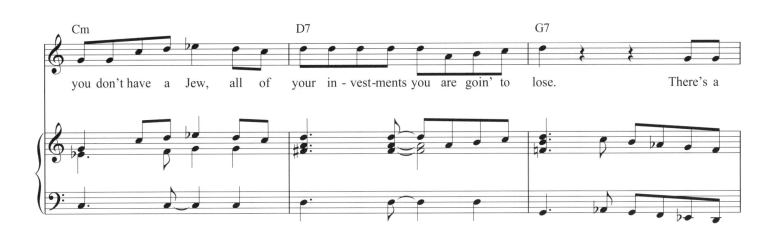

you don't have a Jew, all of your in - vest-ments you are goin' to lose. There's a

ver - y small per - cen - tile who en - joys a danc-ing gen - tile. I'm sad to be the one with this bad

SANTA FE

from Disney's *Newsies The Musical*
(Broadway Version)

Music by Alan Menken
Lyrics by Jack Feldman

Folks, we fi-n'lly got a head-line: "New-sies crushed as bulls at-tack!" Crutch-ie's call-in' me, dumb

crip's just too damn slow. Guys are

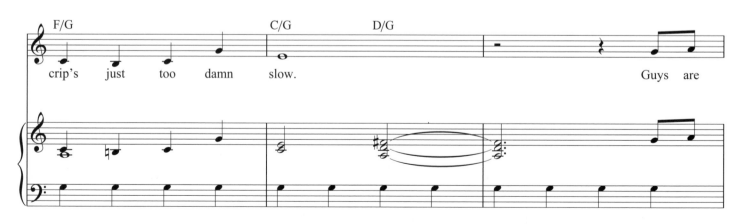

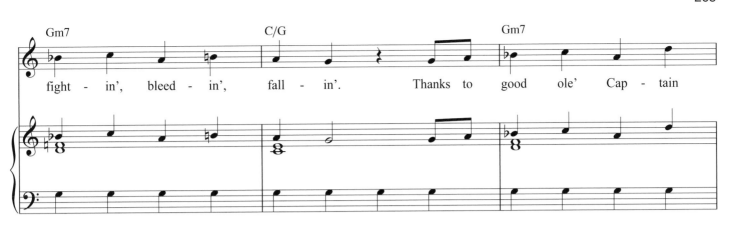

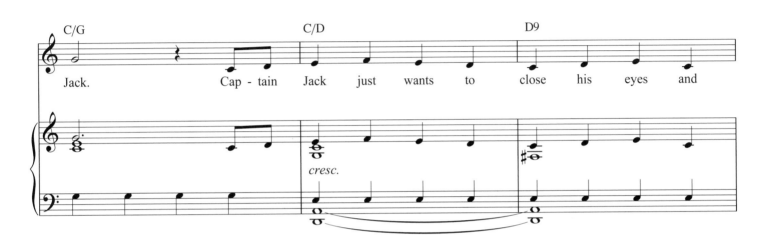

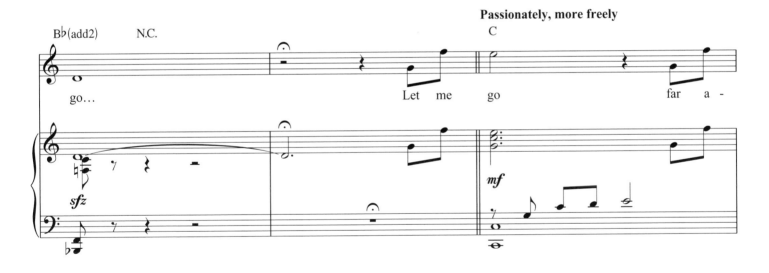

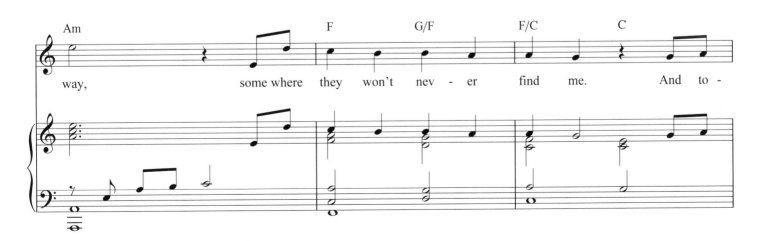

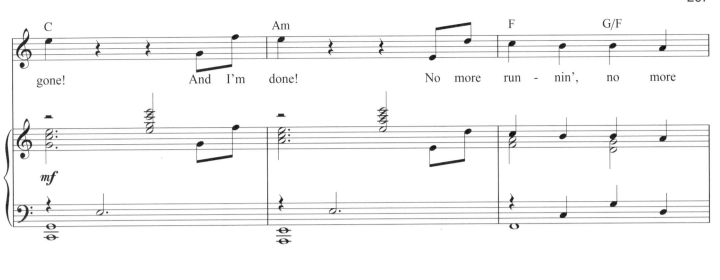

gone! And I'm done! No more run-nin', no more

ly - in'. No more fat old men de-ny-ing me my

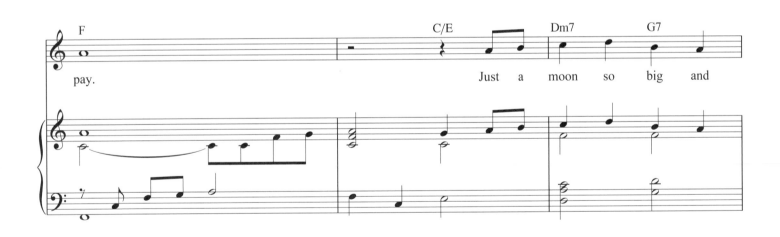

pay. Just a moon so big and

yel - low, it turns night right in - to day. Dreams come

With more drive

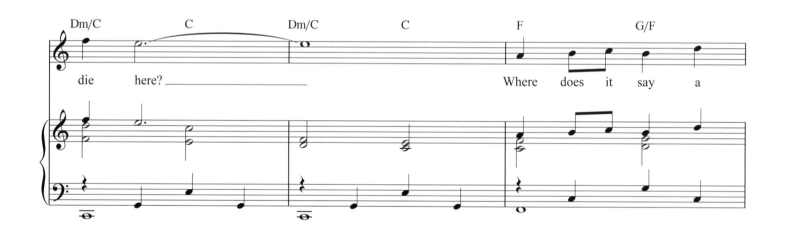

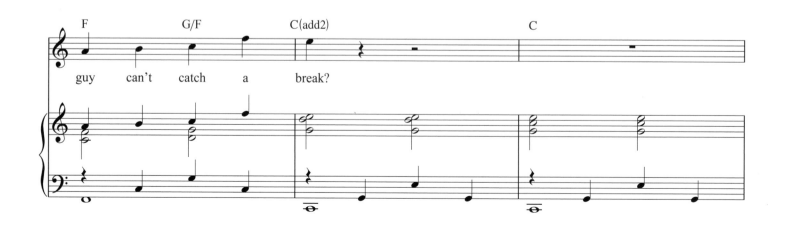

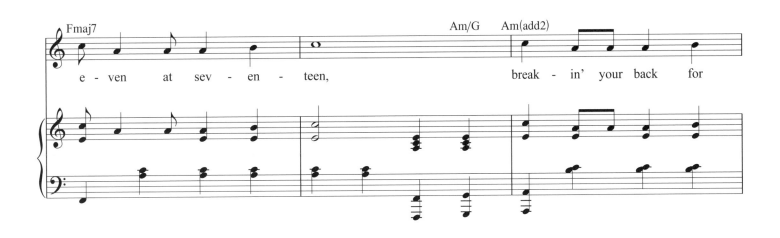

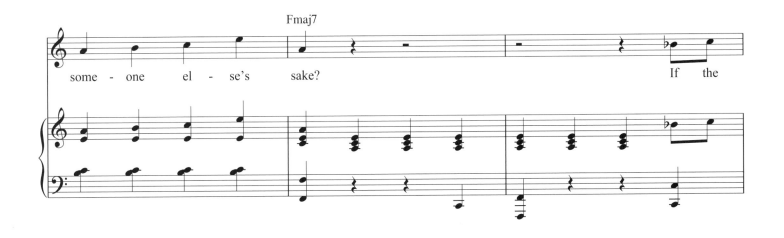

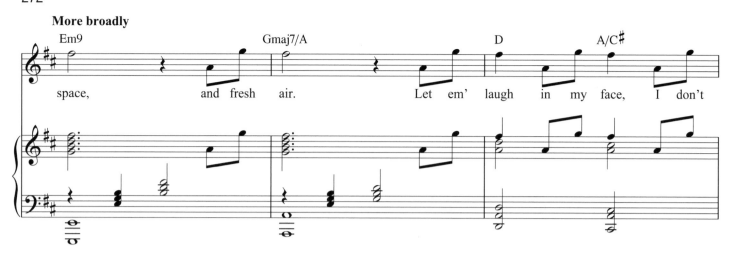

More broadly

space, and fresh air. Let em' laugh in my face, I don't

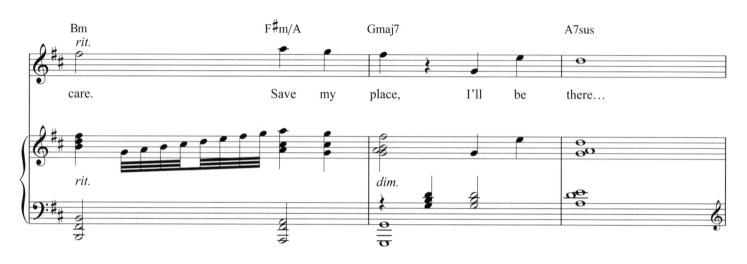

care. Save my place, I'll be there…

A tempo (poco rubato)

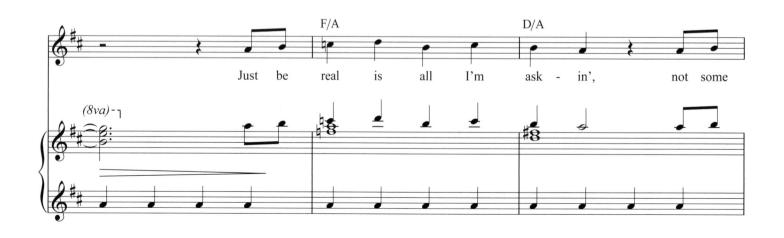

Just be real is all I'm ask - in', not some

THERE'S A WORLD
from *Next to Normal*

Lyrics by Brian Yorkey
Music by Tom Kitt

LEAVE
from the Motion Picture *Once*

Words and Music by
Glen Hansard

Slowly, in 1, swing ($\quad$ = 140)

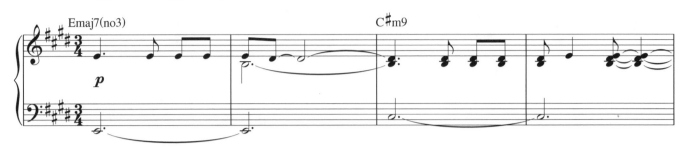

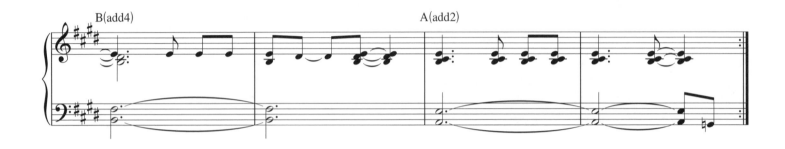

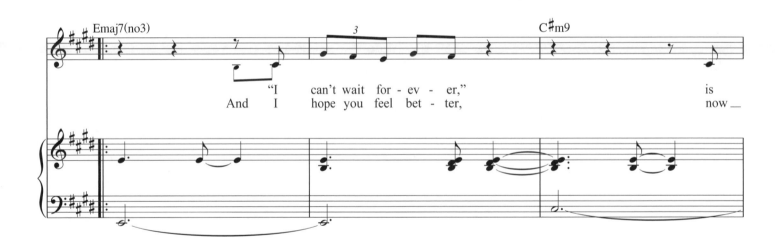

SAY IT TO ME NOW

from the Motion Picture *Once*

Words and Music by Glen Hansard,
Graham Downey, Paul Brennan,
Noreen O'Donnell, Colm Macconiomaire
and David Odlum

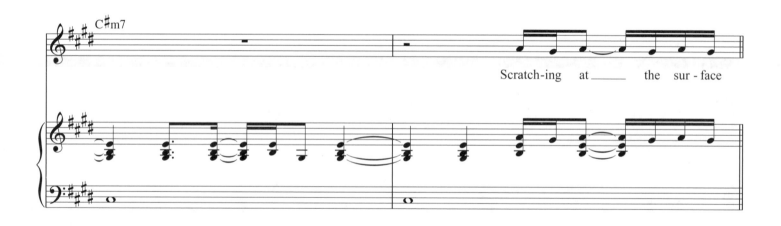

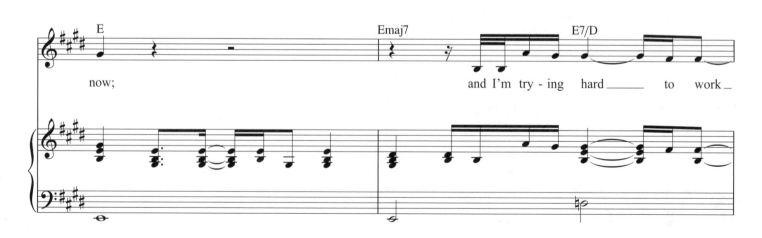

it out.

And so much has gone mis-un-der-

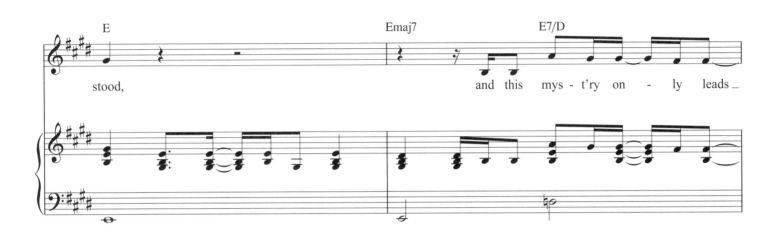

stood,

and this mys-t'ry on - ly leads

to doubt.

And I did-n't un-der-stand,

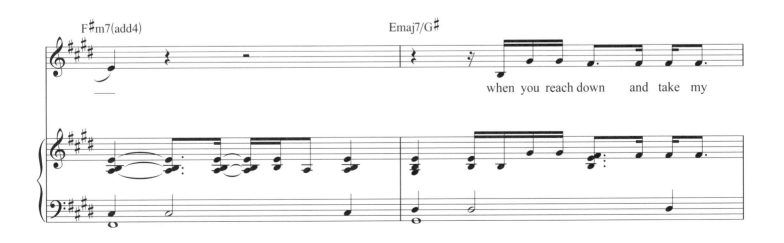

when you reach down and take my

This page has been intentionally left blank to facilitate page turns.

WHEN YOUR MIND'S MADE UP

from the Motion Picture *Once*

Words and Music by
Glen Hansard

SPRINGTIME FOR HITLER
from *The Producers*

Music and Lyrics by
Mel Brooks

STORM TROOPER:

Ger-ma-ny was hav-ing trou-ble, what a sad, sad sto-ry,

need-ed a new lead-er to re-store its for-mer glo-ry.

Where, oh where, was he? Where could that man be? We

The Storm Trooper introduces the song in this production number, which has been adapted as a solo.

Hit - ler and Ger - ma - ny means that soon we'll

be go - ing to war!

ff

This page has been intentionally left blank to facilitate page turns.

WHEN I CLIMB TO THE TOP OF MOUNT ROCK

from *School of Rock*

Music by Andrew Lloyd Webber
Lyrics by Glenn Slater

CODA

Slower

'round the top of Mount Rock.

dim.

The doub- ters and the hat - ers and the

mp

hip - sters let 'em laugh. Soon they'll all be beg - gin' for my

road - ie's au - to - graph. I know my time is com - in', well,

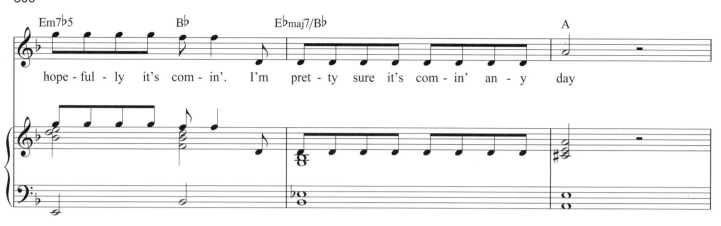

hope-ful-ly it's com-in'. I'm pret-ty sure it's com-in' an-y day

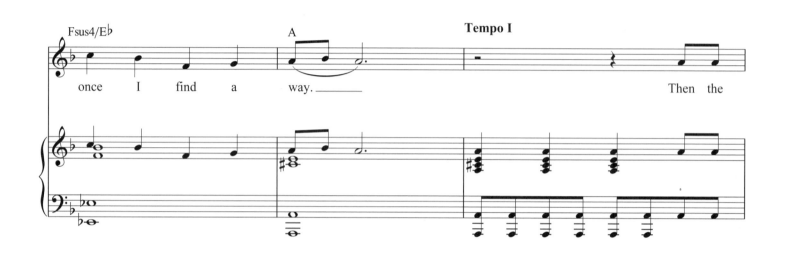

once I find a way. ___ Then the

dreams that I've had ___ since the day I turned ten ___ will be fi-nal-ly com-in' true. ___

And no one will call ___ me a los-er a-gain ___ or

beer.　And　we'll　jam　'round　the　clock

at　the　top　of　Mount　Rock.　At　the　top　of　Mount

Rock.　At　the　top　of　Mount　Rock!

HARD TO BE THE BARD
from *Something Rotten!*

Words and Music by
Wayne Kirkpatrick
and Karey Kirkpatrick

Sing Shakepeare's part only for a solo version.

pose for a por-trait, and how I de-plore sit-ting there for e - ter - ni - ty.___ Then it's

off to the inn, where my inn-keep-er friend wants to name a drink af-ter me! Then it's

back to my room where I re-sume__ my at-tempt to write a hit.___ Just

me and my beer and the ter-ri-ble fear that___ I might be los-ing it. And it's

(Drums)

SHAKESPEARE: *I know writing made me famous,*
but being famous is just so much more fun.

write down a word, but it's NOT the right word, so you TRY a new word, but you HATE the new word, then you

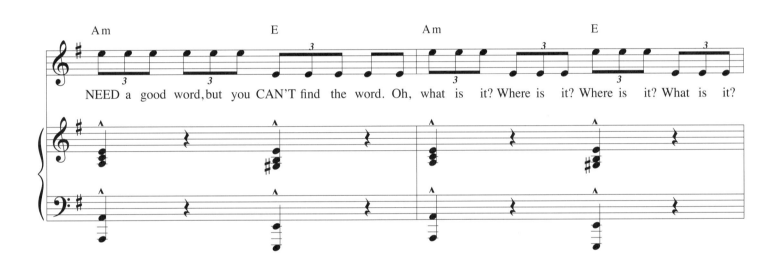

NEED a good word, but you CAN'T find the word. Oh, what is it? Where is it? Where is it? What is it?

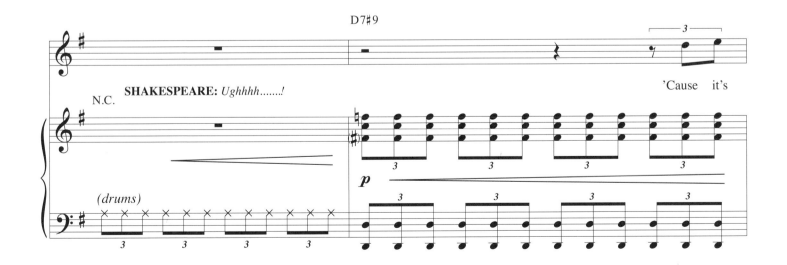

SHAKESPEARE: *Ughhhh.......!*

'Cause it's

A cut has been made for this solo edition.

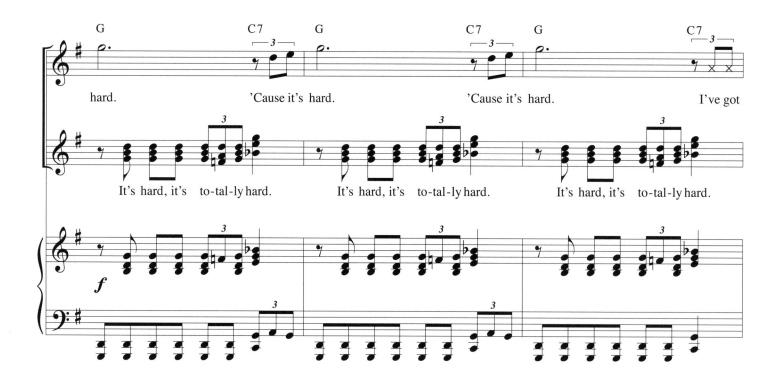

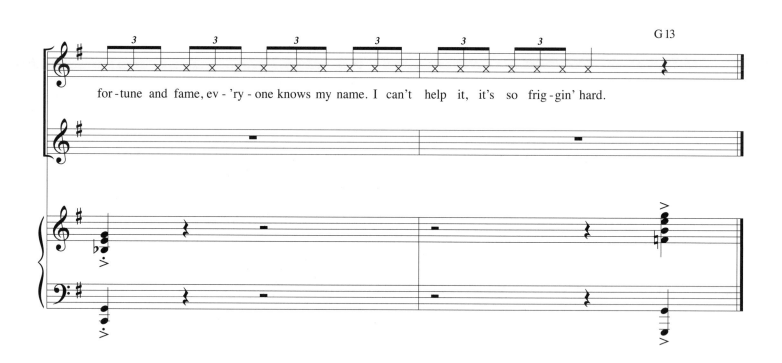

ALL THAT'S KNOWN

from *Spring Awakening*

Words by Steven Sater
Music by Duncan Sheik

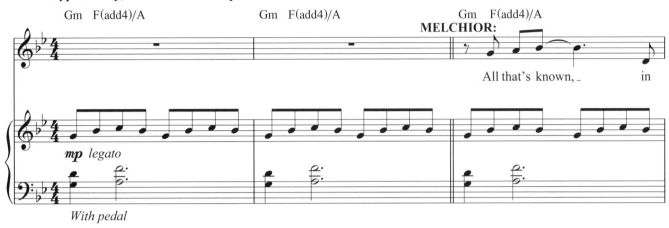

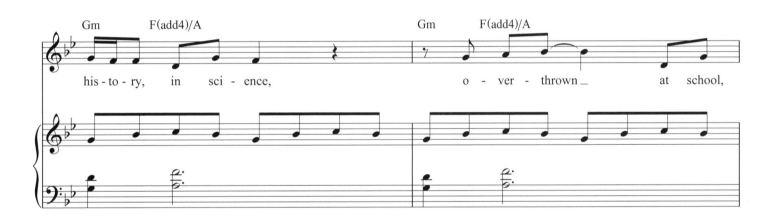

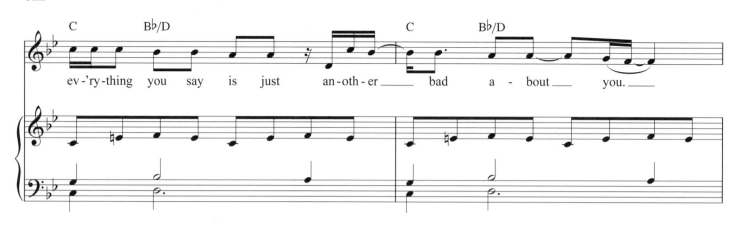

ev-'ry-thing you say is just an-oth-er ____ bad a - bout ____ you. ____

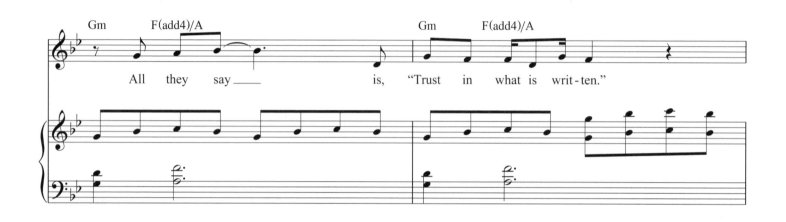

All they say ____ is, "Trust in what is writ-ten."

Wars are made, ____ and some - how that is wis - dom.

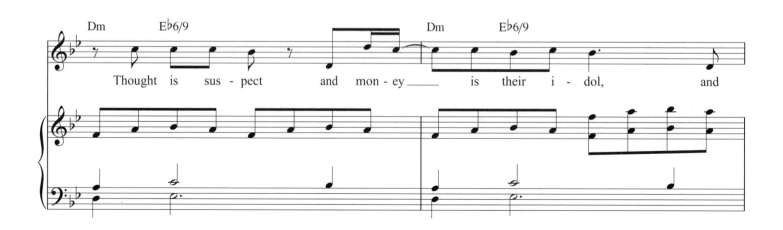

Thought is sus - pect and mon-ey ____ is their i - dol, and

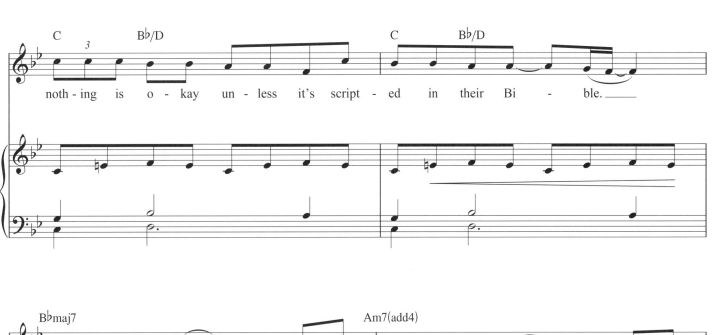

noth-ing is o-kay un-less it's script-ed in their Bi - ble. ____

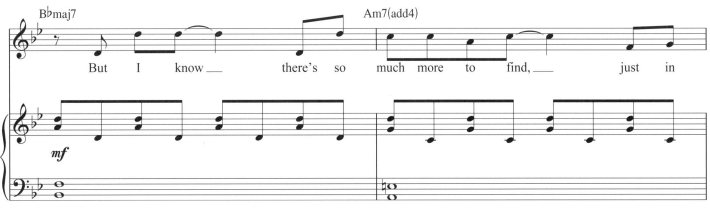

But I know ____ there's so much more to find, ____ just in

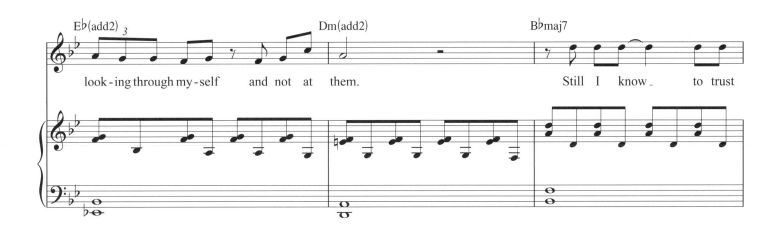

look-ing through my-self and not at them. Still I know ___ to trust

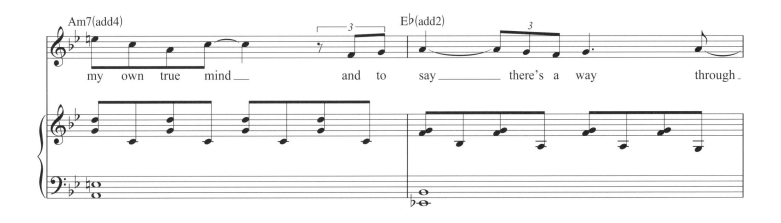

my own true mind ___ and to say _____ there's a way through __

You watch — me, just watch — me. I'm

call - ing, — and one day all will know. — You watch — me,

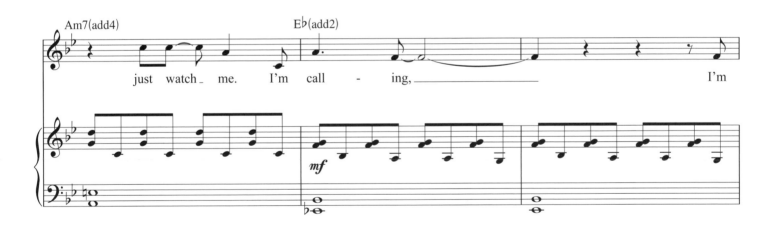

just watch — me. I'm call - ing, ——————————— I'm

call - ing, — and one — day all — will know... —

LEFT BEHIND
from *Spring Awakening*

Music by Duncan Sheik
Lyrics by Steven Sater

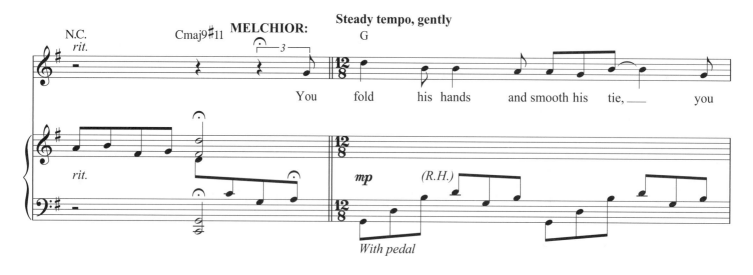

You fold his hands and smooth his tie, ___ you gen-tly lift his chin. _ Were you real-ly so blind and un-kind _ to him? Can't help the itch to touch, to kiss, to

ONE TRACK MIND
from the Broadway Musical *Sweet Smell of Success*

Music by Marvin Hamlisch
Lyric by Craig Carnelia

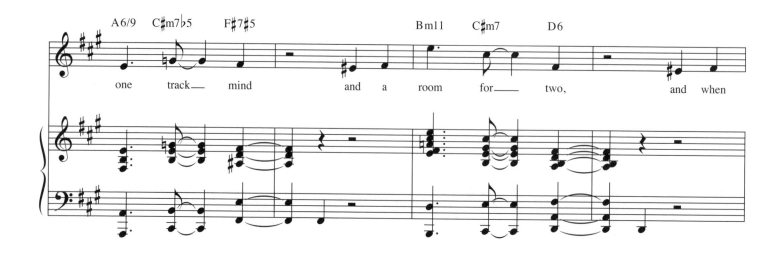

WHAT DO I NEED WITH LOVE

from *Thoroughly Modern Millie*

Music by Jeanine Tesori
Lyrics by Dick Scanlan

Freely, conversational

JIMMY: *mp*

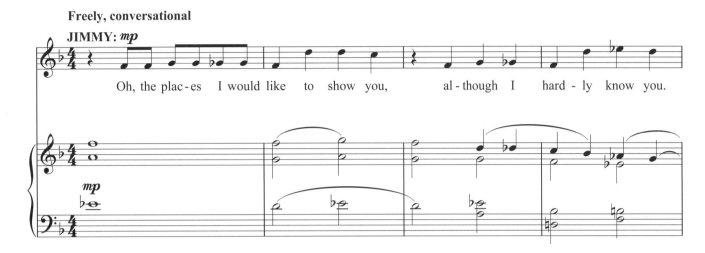

Oh, the plac-es I would like to show you, al-though I hard-ly know you.

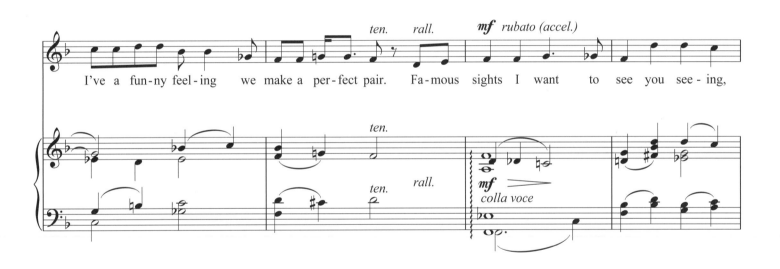

I've a fun-ny feel-ing we make a per-fect pair. Fa-mous sights I want to see you see-ing,

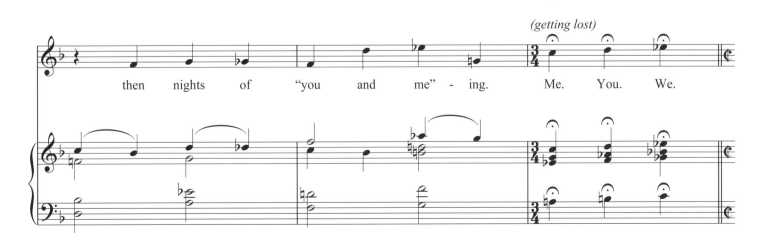

then nights of "you and me"-ing. Me. You. We.

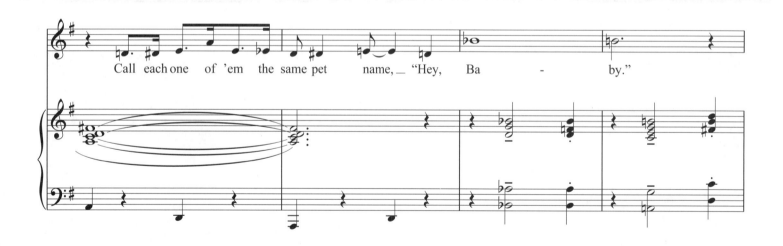

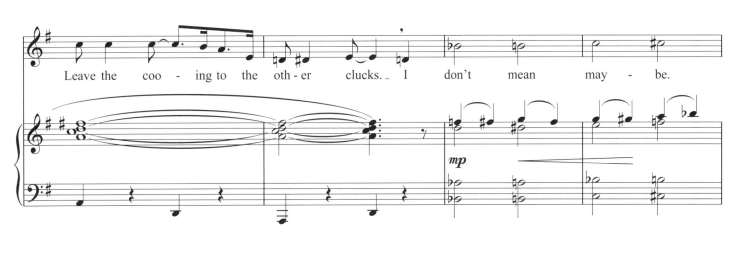

Leave the coo - ing to the oth - er clucks. __ I don't mean may - be.

Got it good. __ What do I need __ with love?

Al - ways prac - tice what I preach: __ keep temp - ta - tion out of eas - y reach. __

Stick to dolls who wash their hair in bleach, __ I'm __ hap - py.

Come and go the way I choose. _ Nev - er gon - na sing the

tied down blues. _ Oth - er guys _ would kill to fill my shoes. _ No

wing - clipped sap - py! Got it good. _ What do I need _ with

love? _ That was a near miss.

Got it good.___ What do I need___ with love?___

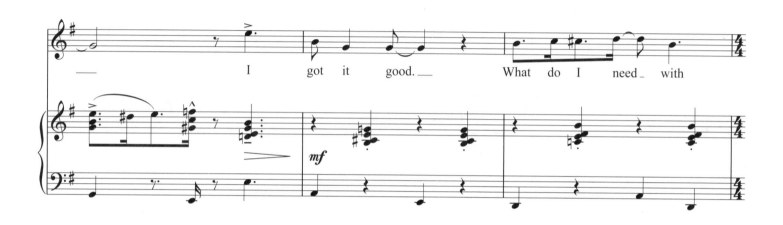

___ I got it good.___ What do I need___ with

Double time feel - Straight 8ths

"Jolson"

love?___ Skip the vows and

all that rot.___ Tell the min-is-ter that "I___ do"___ not.

Bright and breez-y is the... Birds and bee-sy is the... Free and eas-y is the

life I got with - out her.

Freely, slowly *rit.* *rit.*

Al - though I hard - ly know you...

p gently

Swing! *f*

What do I need with love? _____ I

This page has been intentionally left blank to facilitate page turns.

MY UNFORTUNATE ERECTION

from *The 25th Annual Putnam County Spelling Bee*

Words and Music by
William Finn

This page has been intentionally left blank to facilitate page turns.

DANCING THROUGH LIFE

from the Broadway Musical *Wicked*

Music and Lyrics by
Stephen Schwartz

The trou-ble with schools is____ they al-ways try to teach the wrong les-son.____ Be-lieve me, I've been kicked out of e-nough of them___ to know.____ They want you to be-come less cal-low, less shal-low, but I say, "Why in-vite

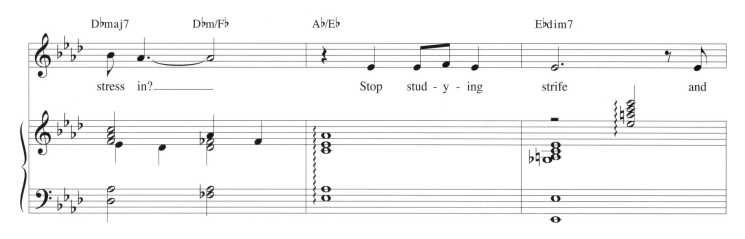

stress in?_____ Stop stud - y - ing strife and

Pop "Dance beat"

learn to live 'the un - ex - am - ined life'"..._____

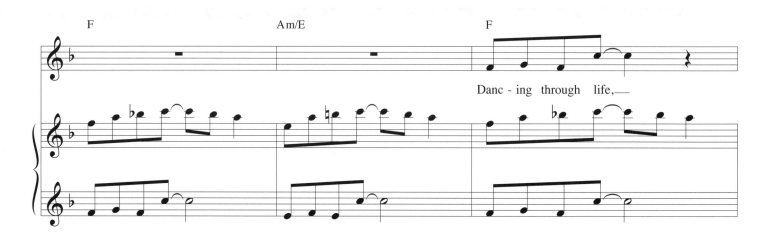

Danc - ing through life,____

skim - ming the sur - face, glid - ing where turf____ is smooth._____

WONDERFUL
from the Broadway Musical *Wicked*

Music and Lyrics by
Stephen Schwartz

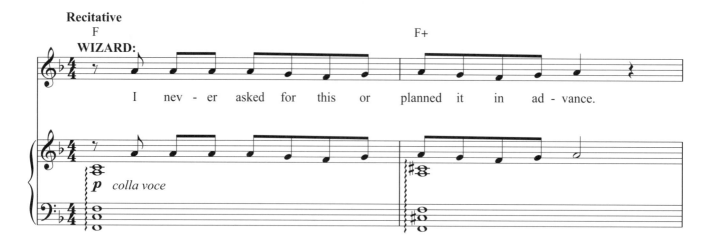

I never asked for this or planned it in advance.

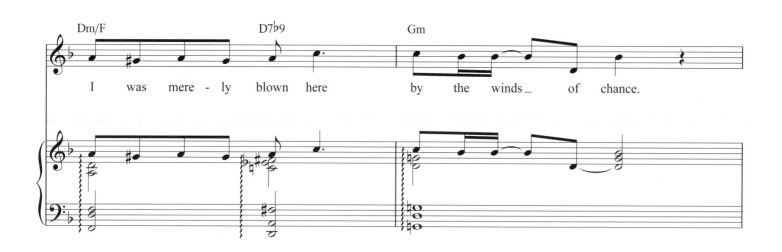

I was merely blown here by the winds of chance.

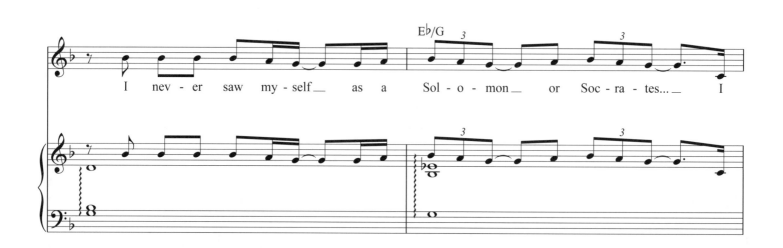

I never saw myself as a Sol-o-mon or Soc-ra-tes... I

Where I come from, we believe all sorts of things that aren't true—we call it..."history."

I'LL BE HERE

from *The Wild Party*

Words and Music by
Andrew Lippa

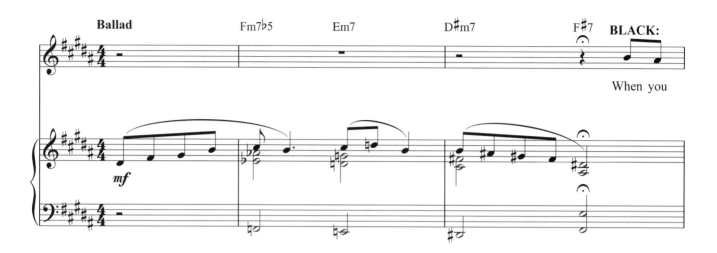

WHAT IS IT ABOUT HER?
from *The Wild Party*

Words and Music by
Andrew Lippa

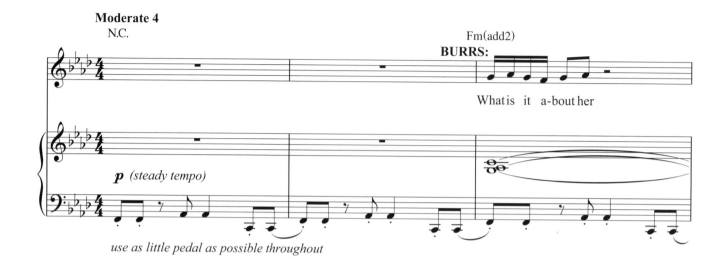

This song is a duet for Burrs and Queenie in the show, adapted here as a solo.

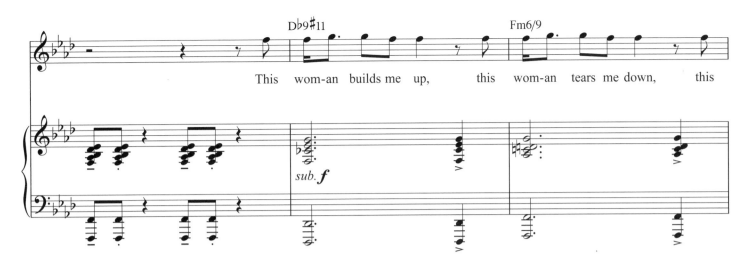

This wom-an builds me up, this wom-an tears me down, this

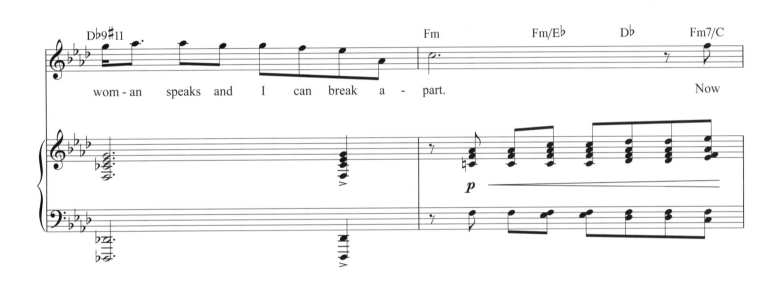

wom-an speaks and I can break a-part. Now

comes an-oth-er man pre-tend-ing he can win her heart, well,

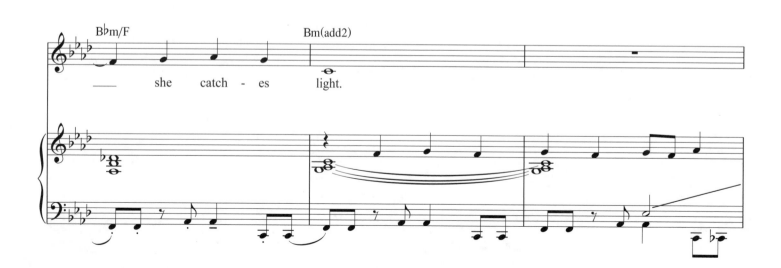

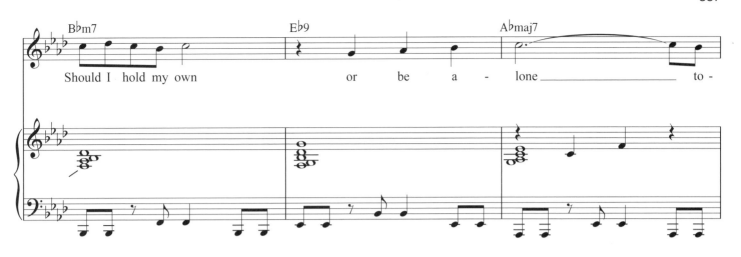

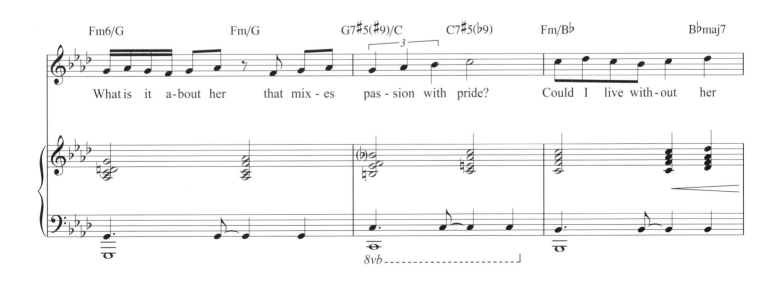

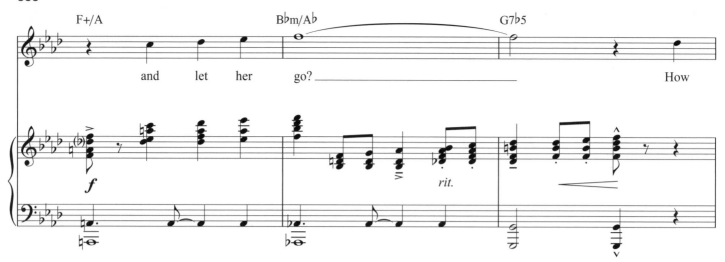

and let her go? _____ How

loud   must   I   scream   NO! _____

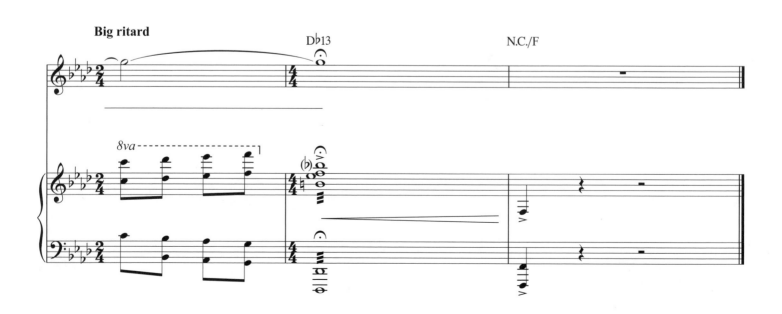

This page has been intentionally left blank to facilitate page turns.

ONE KNIGHT
from the Broadway Musical *Wonderland*

Music by Frank Wildhorn
Lyrics by Jack Murphy

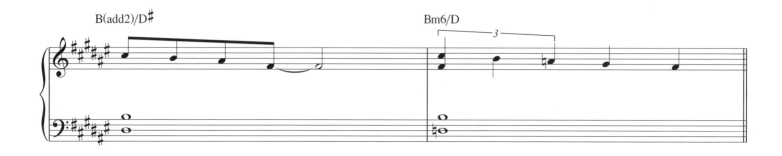

JACK:
Give me a drag-on I can slay. Just say the word and I'll o-bey.

Show me a dam-sel in dis-tress, and I'll save her.

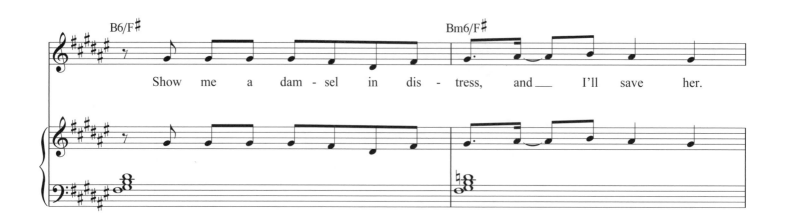

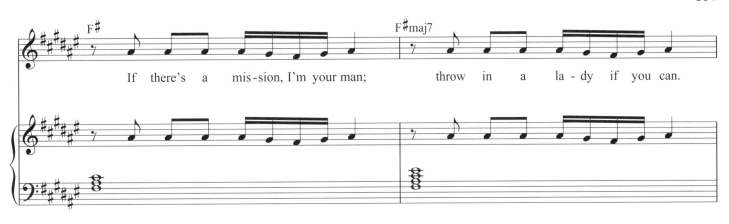

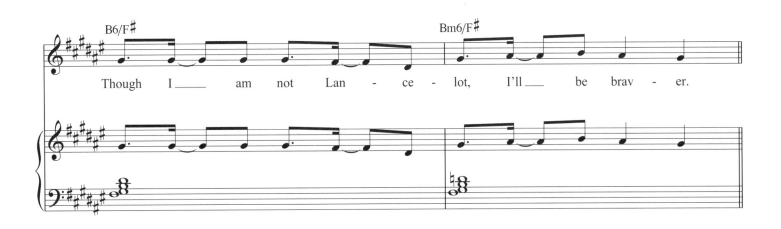

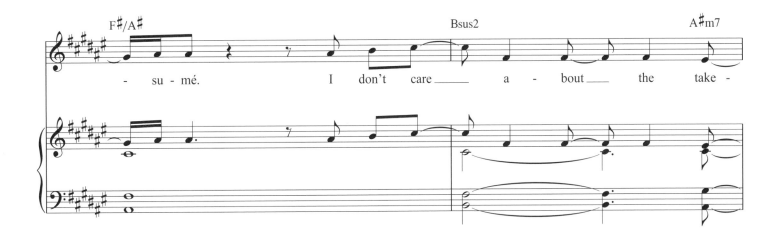